HELICOPTERS

Please visit our web site at: www.garethstevens.com
For a free color catalog describing Gareth Stevens Publishing's
list of high-quality books and multimedia programs,
call 1-800-542-2595 or fax your request to (414) 332-3567.

Library of Congress Cataloging-in-Publication Data available upon request from publisher.
Fax (414) 336-0157 for the attention of the Publishing Records Department.

ISBN 0-8368-3046-6

First published in 2002 by
Gareth Stevens Publishing
A World Almanac Education Group Company
330 West Olive Street, Suite 100
Milwaukee, WI 53212 USA

Text and photos: Eric Ethan
Cover design and page layout: Tammy Gruenewald

This edition © 2002 by Gareth Stevens, Inc.

Printed in the United States of America

1 2 3 4 5 6 7 8 9 06 05 04 03 02

EMERGE
VEHICLES

by Eric Ethan

Gareth Stevens Publishing
A WORLD ALMANAC EDUCATION GROUP COMPANY

This is a medical rescue helicopter. It can quickly take sick or injured people to the hospital.

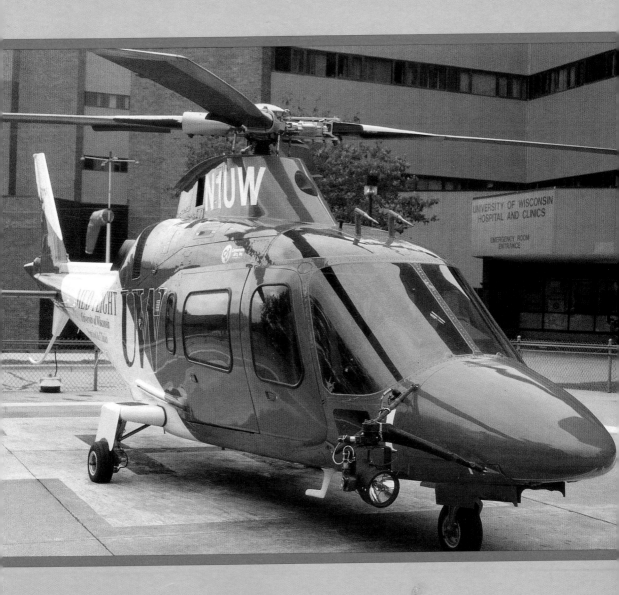

A medical helicopter has special equipment on it. This equipment is used to take care of patients until they reach the hospital.

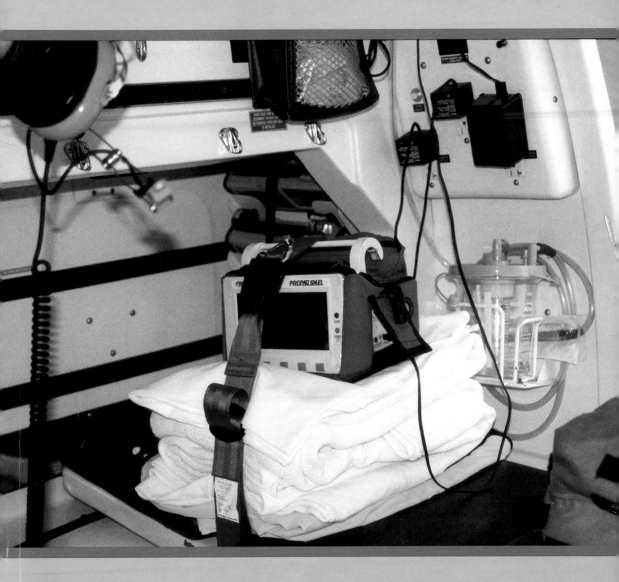

The helicopter has a crew. The crew includes a pilot and a flight nurse.

The pilot sits in the cockpit to fly the helicopter. The cockpit has many switches and dials.

The pilot can land the helicopter close to a hospital. A white cross shows the pilot where to land.

The flight nurse sits close to the patient when the helicopter is flying. He or she gives medical care during the flight to the hospital. The flight nurse wears headphones and safety belts.

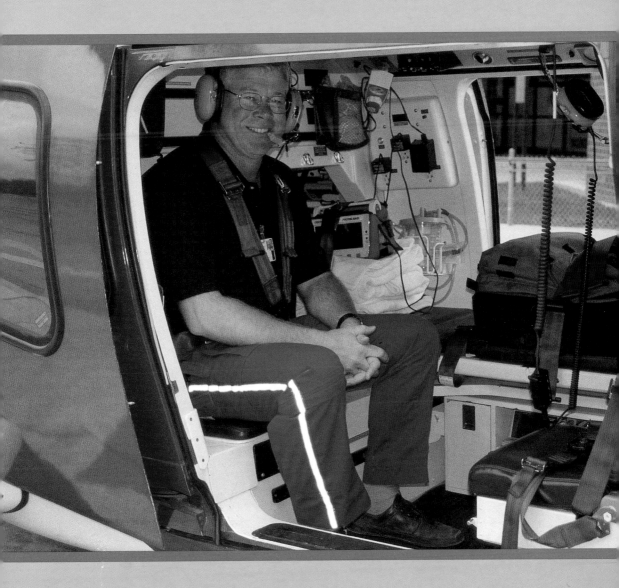

The helicopter has more places to sit if another nurse or doctor is needed.

A dispatcher uses a radio to talk to the helicopter's crew. The dispatcher tells the crew where to go and what kind of help is needed.

This helicopter and its crew
are on their way!

GLOSSARY

cockpit (KAHK-pit): the place where the pilot sits to control an airplane or helicopter.

crew (kroo): a group of people who work together.

equipment (ee-KWIP-ment): the tools a person uses to do a job.

medical (MED-ih-kul): having to do with healing or giving out medicine.

patient (PAY-shunt): a person who is being taken care of by doctors or nurses.

MORE BOOKS TO READ

Rescue Helicopters. Hal Rogers (The Child's World)

Rescue Helicopters. Transportation Library (series). Becky Olien (Bridgestone Books)

Working Hard with the Rescue Helicopter. Cynthia Benjamin (Scholastic)

WEB SITES

Alec Buck's EMS Helicopters
www.alecbuck.com

Northland's Rescue Helicopter
www.northlandhelicopter.co.nz/index.htm

INDEX